GLAZED WITH WAR

PANTEA AMIN TOFANGCHI

MASON JAR PRESS | BALTIMORE, MD

Cover design and layout by Ian Anderson. Cover art provided by the author.

This book is set in Meta Serif Pro and Milkstore.

Publishded by
Mason Jar Press
Baltimore, MD

Printed by Spencer Printing in Honesdale, PA.

Learn more about Mason Jar Press at masonjarpress.com.

for my family you are my نورونفس

for my mountains Alborz and Dena, when this book was published you were in the second grade, I was in the second grade when the war started. How many pomegranate seeds are we different from one another? Too many, one might say. Not too many, if we think of our world as one big country.

for my friends, without you this journey would have been impossible.

for my people, may you live in peace someday.
And for all the war children in the world.

AN INTRODUCTION

Every experience we have is as unique as it is universal. Pantea Amin Tofangchi's memoir-in-poems is about a very specific war—the Iran–Iraq War that lasted from September 1980 to August 1988—and it is experienced from the singular perspective of an Iranian girl; yet it speaks to shared experience through the very engine of its specificity. How does a child live through something as devastating as war? How does a child live through any trauma? Quite simply, she lives. She eats. She sleeps. She goes to school. She even plays. She folds the fabric of the trauma into her daily life, and carries it into adulthood and the world.

Memory has a face, she says, and in reading Pantea's childhood remembrances of acacia trees and the *turquoise of the Persian Gulf,* I'm reminded of syringa trees and the azure of the Atlantic Ocean in Southern Africa. When she writes, *Like petals / or wildflowers in the mountain / some of our friends just left / to live in other lands,* I think of how in time—in different ways—so did we, she and I.

Her leaving was to turn away from war, from the oppression of women, from uprisings violently subdued by her government. My turning away was more ephemeral; it was from remorse and shame for a government that devised the word and ethos of *apartheid*. Yet, for all our difference, Pantea and I found commonality in our outsider-insider status—our *apartness*—as naturalized Americans in our adopted country.

For both of us, our leaving was predicated on having come of age in our dysfunctional countries.

But, as Pantea's grandfather tells her, *There is no such thing / as an easy country*. This is true of Iran, of South Africa, of America, of any country. And to read how Pantea's young life was *Glazed With War* is to lend perspective to every war, like the latter-day conflict in Ukraine, and to share her outrage:

> *Nobody admitted the mistake.*
> *Politicians usually don't.*
> *That war was not a mistake.*
> *This war isn't either!*
> *These wars aren't*
> *The ones that haven't happened yet,*

In each observation, Pantea opens the door to empathy. As I have felt its resonance, so you will find your own.

Judith Krummeck, 2023
writer | broadcaster | immigrant

POEMS

Many things in the world have
already happened. You can
go back and tell about them.
They are part of what we
own as we speed along
through the white sky."

—William Stafford

بنی‌آدم اعضای یک دیگرند
که در آفرینش ز یک گوهرند
چو عضوی به‌درد آورَد روزگار
دگر عضوها را نمانَد قرار
تو کز محنت دیگران بی‌غمی
نشاید که نامت نهند آدمی

—Saadi

MY MAHOGANY PALACE
A PRELUDE:

to all the war-children in the world

so I flew back in time

again

to the loud noises
the cracks
the masking tapes
to the candlelight flashlight
to my father's small black radio
to our basement filled
    with cans dry fruits tissues blankets batteries
    water bottles towels soap bars band-aids medicines
    along with agony worry and broken hearts
to a black war and a gray peace —

under the mahogany dining table
I hear my heavy breathing when the attacks were starting
I remember
I let the air fly to my lungs with my eyes closed
I remember the smell
of the big dark-brown blanket
my mother would throw over the table
so the light of the flashlight wouldn't show through

no light after dark in our Tehran
not even a spark
not from any house
no street lamps
not even a lightening bug
where were the stars
the moon and shooting stars
I wonder —

eight years old I was
under the dining table under the big brown blanket

doing
my homework
holding
the red and white flashlight
my parents still have it

this is jang it may last 10 years they have to sleep in their rooms
my father said slowly

I looked at them quietly
through the part my mom left open
for air to flow
the mattresses already
waiting for us to dive in
my mom was covering them with sheets
this isn't just war

said my mom with a shaky voice
this is marg and
if we have to die I want us to die together
she said
and I saw two giant pearls falling down her cheek

taking the red pencil out of my little sister's
little hand
I whispered
natars natars don't be afraid don't be afraid
she is not crying she is just allergic to the dust
I lied
and I put the red pencil on her innocent flower on the white paper

when is this war going to end
I asked my dad

never he whispered to himself so suddenly

he turned toward me
and kissed my forehead
soon baba joon
soon

GLAZED WITH WAR

IN SECOND GRADE

The war started
and we carried it
like an unexpected rain
weighted down wet and thick
we carried ourselves every morning
heavy,
firebrick in our backpacks.

It was there,
part of our routine:
anti-aircraft sounds,
sirens, تصمیم کبری
fear, حسنک کجایی
bombs and death.

But at eight
carrying a bag filled
with pencils: red and black
eraser, pencil sharpener, ruler
napkins and a foldable cup
an apple, feta cheese and walnut sandwich
along with war
was normal to me.

CARTOON TIME

Again?!

everyday
the power outage
along with the stupid
war
has to happen on
cartoon time?

I exclaimed to my mom!

I wish . . .
(the sound of anti-aircraft guns were loud, so I started to yell)

can't they just bomb
in the mornings?

THE BLUE HEADLIGHT

The cars
aren't made with pale blue
headlights.
Later, I learned that
people painted them blue
so the enemy couldn't
spot them from thousands of miles away.

THE MASKING TAPE

Today
all our school windows
are decorated
with masking tape
thick grayish brown
X
on all windows
keeps us safe, says the teacher
from shattered glass
in case the bomb misses the school and
the sound wave doesn't.
I think حسن آقا
did them all.
He does everything,
from plumbing to changing the light bulb.
We are safe now.

THE EGLANTINE ROSE

at eight
supposedly innocent,
we would walk back home
from school often
in groups of five or six

which one seemed more important
to an eight-year-old girl with cream and brown school uniform?

the house whose front yard door was covered
with pink Eglantine Roses

or a woman yelling
kids it's red siren, run to your houses

I stopped,
to steal a rose for my mama.

RELIGIOUS STUDIES

Whatever was going on
in my head at eight
still lives in me

She said we were free
to ask her any questions
regarding religion.

I must have raised
my small hand,
Where did God come from?

She looked at me
with a thick white silence
don't ever ask that question of anybody!

ASH-RAINS

it rained
ashes those days

there are still some
black spots on me

in my pocket lives
a bird that can swim

all the way back
to my second grade
one day,
lifting me up

light like a feather,
to the 4th street by the school

another day
leaving me behind a thick black fog,

close enough
to smell it all again

ashes ashes
ashes ashes

IT'S STILL THERE

we were there

learning one word at a time
making short sentences with new words
memorizing little skinny poems
appropriate for our age
simple history lessons
            nothing bad lasts,
we would learn
simple religion lessons
            God loves everybody,
he loves Saddam too?
and the pilots who release
the button full of bombs?

it was there
the war
and its bitterness
we were all there . . .

I WONDER IF MOM REMEMBERS

I remember when it was dropped
On میدان مادر, mother square.
It felt as if all our windows
came out.
We couldn't believe that
nothing was broken
(a few picture frames never counted)

and I remember
reporting my school day to my mom the day after:

my friend's sister and her dad were there
and before she said anything I continued

they saw a man crying over the remains
of his wife's pregnant body
the baby's remains were scattered around mother square

She didn't say anything
how could she?

They are still there, they say
The don't have enough people to
Clean up
People are helping

Can we go to help?

She was mute.

Her silence perhaps
changed my curiosity to ire

God is not great,
I finally said.
He is actually very stupid, I cried.

It all started then,
my relationship with God
was never cured.

THE ROUND WINDOW

Sunrise in September used to be cold.

The smell of نارنگی نوبر
the sound of a teaspoon dancing
in the large teacup
while my Papa sweetened his tea,
our dark kitchen, my mama, my dad, my baby sister, Nader.

Memory has a face.
Memory is thin and sharp.

I see me
standing on the street corner
looking up at our apartment.

What if I go to school
and our home is gone
while I'm gone too?

There stands my mama
her face, smiling at me
through the round window
among the green leaves
the school is a few blocks away
doesn't matter whether the bomb drops

on our home or your school
we will be still together, she tells me.

I throw her kisses.
she always stays until
I disappear.

CHOCOLATE ARMY

We would line up before class
in the yard.
Single line for each class,
first graders' lines then the second graders'
Like a petite army
in brown and cream uniforms
caramel and chocolate,
yin and yang
innocence vs. war.

Then they would talk:
Our principal, sometimes other people too
When it was our turn to speak up
all of us would start screaming at her signal:

WAR WAR TILL VICTORY
WAR WAR TILL VICTORY
WAR WAR TILL VICTORY
WAR WAR TILL VICTORY

for years
that's how we started our mornings.

I WISH WE DIDN'T HAVE OIL

There is no such thing
as an easy country.
my grandfather Papa replied.
What about those
that do not have oil, natural gas
diamonds, minerals
a lot of wheat and rice,
those who do not have
something that makes
other countries wealthy?
They live in fear, my sweet girl.
In fear of what?
Of those who have, because you see
we depend on one another.

He used to put his fingers
on his chin while he was talking.
He discussed the war with me treated me as an adult.

ESSAY EXAM

Choose one:
How did you spend your summer?
Describe your favorite season.
Write a letter to a soldier.

~~Dear soldier~~
~~Thanks for killing~~
~~our enemy~~
~~so they don't kill us.~~
~~How can I serve my country, I once asked my teacher.~~
~~I am a girl~~
~~and I am too young to kill~~
~~and too young to get killed. (I don't mind dying though)~~
~~My teacher pointed at my pencil and said~~
~~you are serving your country, with this pencil.~~
~~I hope you come back~~
~~home to your family soon.~~
~~I hope your house is still there and everybody~~
~~in your family is alive.~~
~~dear sol~~

Autumn, red, orange, yellow
and brown fall comes in many colors.
Rain —

LIBERATION OF KHORRAMSHAHR

The sound
stays longer,
the voice,
the spoken words
I can hear tulips and
palm trees thousands of miles away in the south
I can even hear اروندرود
if I listen closely

That day
in those gloomy foggy
days of war and innocence
I was in my grandfather's room, sitting on his bed
watching برنامه کودکان و نوجوانان on the TV
when it got interrupted:

هموطنان عزیز توجه فرمایید!
my fellow countrymen, may I have your attention
هموطنان عزیز توجه فرمایید!
dear listeners, may I have your attention please!
my fellow Iranians, may I have your attention please!

not once, not twice
he repeated those lines
many times

I was nine,
the background music
a march — still too familiar in my head

my fellow countrymen

خرمشهر،
شهر خون
آزاد شد

Khorramshahr,
the city of blood
is freed.

زنگ پرورشی

Who knows about عملیات ولفجر۵
We looked at her puzzled
Nobody?
Operation valfajr 5 was
Blah blah blah
Blah blah blah
Blah blah blah
I think at the end
some good guys killed
many bad guys and a few
good guys got killed
do you know how lucky you are
living in the capital, she said.
In the cities near the borders
many children are dead
many are without
houses, schools, parents and families.

It felt like she was mad at us.
It felt as if it was not right to
have parents and schools and to be alive, all at the same time.
It felt like
I was lucky.
Someone else's loss was my luck
and I believed her.
I *was* lucky.

THE BLOOD CITY

This is Shahrzad
our teacher said
she's your new classmate.
She's from Khoramshahr.

She did not say
that her family had lost
their house
their city was gone
but we knew

YOU WEREN'T HERE

Close to where the sun rose
A few houses down
Lived a long apartment building
Dedicated to the war victims of the Abadan & Khorramshahr
Hurt
Different
Pour, most of them once rich
Kind
Messy, angry, decent, sad and dark
Those who lost everything but their bodies
"the lucky ones."

Some said
in each room lived many families
families that once had
huge houses and beautiful lives
among oleanders and palms
close to endless turquoise of the Persian Gulf

among them lived a man
who was mentally damaged during the war,
          who wasn't?
But he, more than the rest of them in that building.
I never had the guts to ask him who
how, what and how many had he lost

After the liberation of Khorramshahr
he carried a small cassette tape player
in a red plastic grocery basket
that was always on.
He cried and walked our street
back and forth for
days, months, maybe years
with one song on loud:

Mammad you weren't here to see
that our city is free

Mammad you weren't here to see
that our city is free

Mammad you weren't here to see
that our city is free

MY TRANSPARENT ROOTS

My reminiscence
of the days we lived in war
are too vivid
A dark chocolate meeting my taste buds,
honey dripping, one long drop on my finger.
The days that left me
with too many questions,
questions we either forgot
or gave up,
or learned to live them.
Had I been a tree,
I would treasure my roots.
had I been a tree,
would I have ever wanted to leave?

DO BOMBS VISIT ALL THE FLOORS?

—for my friend Bahareh who is as beautiful as spring, just like her name

We lived on the second floor
        (eye level with
        the tops of acacia trees)
sometimes we would go to the basement
        (close to the roots)
when we would hear the red siren

somehow it felt safer there
at least for a while
my dad believed it made
no difference in our apartment

        (the life of many
        flowering acacias have
        grown inside me
        like a fear that grew
        inside one's bone)

one of our neighbors in one of our
bomb expecting gatherings in the basement
mentioned that she always feared
being buried alive if we were hit

and I was a mockingbird
mimicking only everybody else's fear
being buried alive, started
my "I want to die in my own room" campaign

my friend at school hated it too
they lived in a very tall high-rise
        (too far from any tree)
traveling all the way
to the basement, often barefoot
and in the middle of the night
in candlelight
with no elevator due to the power outage
was not easy

        (do the trees have memory?
        do they remember?)

THIN US

So thin, the life we had
sometimes I could see inside
my stomach and inside my sister's

the attacks started
we were sitting in the corner of the living room
away from the chandelier, my mom didn't want us
to sit under it when we were under attack

my sister and I, her doll and mine
thin and tight next to one another
looking at our parents who were reading
the newspaper by candlelight
pretending to be relaxed
the life we had
so thin
            in a second, a loud noise
and some other families' lives
thinner than ours,
            ruined.

THICK WATER

There lived a fear in me
that followed me
everywhere.
It grew in me,
in different directions
and it covered
the way I saw my room,
my house, my street,
my city, and beyond.
Hence,
I learned to deal with it.

Leave the door unlocked I would beg my family
as one of them wanted to take a shower
and I would
eagerly
wait
and pray
not to be bombed for another ten minutes or so.

LORD IT OVER

God doesn't exist

I decided one very bomb-heavy day
or maybe he existed at some point
but got killed toward the beginning
of the very first war

مرگ قناری در قفس

—for Nader

فرض کن مرگ قناری در قفس هم مرگ نیست
فرض کن یک شاخه گل هم در جهان هرگز نرست
فرض کن جنگل بیابان بود از روز نخست
در کویری سوت و کور
در میان مردمی با ایز مصیبت ها صبور
صحبت از مرگ محبت مرگ عشق
گفتگو از مرگ انسانیت است

—Fereydoon Moshiri

my canary passed away
he was yellow
and under his neck
he had a thick stripe of lime green
he sang for us
when i greeted him in the mornings
he would chirp back
and when i bent my neck
to the left and right
he would do the same.
it was as if the war didn't matter to him
he was always there

when his mate passed
i wasn't quite as sad

but he stopped
singing
            for a long time

that morning i went to greet him
he was lying dead on his cage floor and i started crying
for many long hours

it rained daisies all over
on my way to school
i felt embarrassed walking
with my friends crying
was it because i was crying
over *joochi* or crying in general

first class was religion
i didn't want to tell my teacher
but my nosy classmate couldn't keep her mouth shut
it seems very silly crying
over a bird when in our country
thousands of innocent people
are being killed everyday
the teacher said
the stupid truth made me
cry harder and harder

i went home still crying
نادر my cousin who lived with us

along with mom and my sister were waiting for me
around the kitchen table
there was a tiny white cardboard casket on the table
lined with cotton, on the white cloudy cotton
lay *joochi* all yellow and lime
i made it for him, said نُدر
he closed the casket with another white cardboard box
on it read in black ink
"we came from him
we go back to him"
the way it's written on the gravestones
then we went out and buried him
and i stopped crying

WAR, SOMETIMES CASUAL

That was not a bomb,
I told my sister so carelessly.
They just broke the sound barrier.

As if she was mistaking
lentils
for split peas.

BLUED DEATH

My grandfather passed
on a Friday
My father's father
we were all there in their house.
He was lying on the bed
I didn't go in.
He had dark blue eyes
gray around the edges.
He loved Hafiz.

They didn't bomb that day.
Or maybe they did
and I didn't notice.

THE RED UMBRELLA

The sound of each drop
on my red umbrella echoed white
like chiffon, soft transparent music in my ears.

A rumble of thunder roared
the sound of my heartbeat rose
and took over the music.

My feet walked faster and faster, my brain bemused.
was it a thunder, an anti-aircraft,
a bomb? Or perhaps a car crashed into an innocent tree?

Then the red siren squealed from Mr. Ali's fruit shop
and I let go of the red umbrella
and ran toward the school

only a block away
but I couldn't reach
my feet were heavy and light at the same time.

At the school gate
our principal grabbed me.
I was a stone running down a hill.

you are OK
you are OK she said.

THE MORNING AFTER

as we were walking to school
we discussed the night before.

I counted 6 bombs, one of us would say.
No, there were 5, one would add
I didn't even wake up, another would say

did we ever talk about
boys, the color of a new backpack,
new tennis shoes, the new movie?
We must have.

BLACK RAINFALL

It rained blackbirds one day
I watched them until my neck was sore.

They are پرستو, swallows, said my aunt.
They are migrating back.
Why, I asked.
Don't they know
there is a war here?

TRANSPARENT COMFORT

Soon this war
will be a bitter memory
I heard my uncle trying to comfort my mom.

If among millions and millions
of houses and apartments
it's our turn to be hit,
so be it.
What can we do?
Let's worry when it happens,
not what if it happens.

What he said stayed with me
a bitter memory
like a music that says sorrow.

POMEGRANATE SKIN

We all have it
more or less
some pieces of childhood
a few thin and thick memories,
mine,
despite all the gray history
my childhood, my friends and family
my beautiful country, have been through
I still remember the taste of ازگیل و زالزالک
and the tray of pomegranates
skinned and گل به گل.
I see myself licking
my tiny fingers
in the candlelight.

ASH MEMORIES

Sandpaper memories
still dust ashes
in the thick air

we are in middle school
all grown-ups now
the war and us

For that we had to wear
our Hejabs in the classroom
of all girls and a female teacher!
It didn't matter,
after all, people were dying
everyday
a piece of fabric on our little heads
was not nearly as bad as a bomb.

BOUNCED THOUGHTS

had i been a bomb
and if and when I hit the ground
i would have flown back up
and fly
that's how i am
i am round, no edges
i contain millions and
millions
of circles.

had i been a boy
i would go too
and fight and help get my country back

as a girl
i
stayed
confused
eager to grow old
eager to forget
a ball too eager to bounce

CHILDHOOD BLUES

As we were growing
older in war
saying goodbye
            to our childhood

was easy.

I didn't even notice.
One day it was gone.
That day I woke up
            a child and went to bed

a grownup.

My classmate's house was hit.
We were so happy the next day
to see her alive.
            Except for the entire family,

everything else was gone.
Thank God, Thank God

we kept saying.

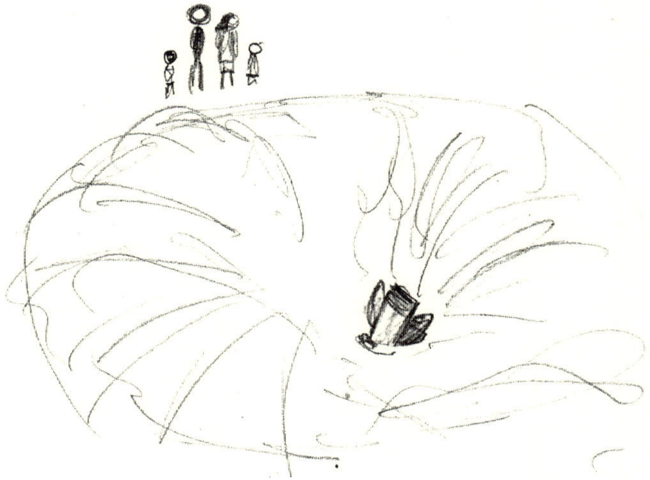

FOOL MOON

Knife night memories
of the nights passed
without any stars
Full moon was our enemy
I thought one night sitting in my bed peeking through
the thick curtain.
Too much light in the dark
could cause the enemy to spot us.
Fool full moon
go and glow
somewhere else.
We do not need your glare,
we are in war.
We have to live in the darkness.

Some of us still do.

HOLLOW MATRIMONY

War on rainy days
was easier to tolerate
thunders and bombs
marrying
under the wet sky.

YELLOW MOON STORY

Once upon a silver morning
there lived a long yellow moon story

of a child who was born on the exact moment
that a bomb was dropped

there was no coincidence, nor was it fate
but people who had faith told the mother that he is a survivor

poor child in this war-race world
my mother sighed in the car

THE EMERALD NIGHT

One dark night
in the corner of our bedroom
my sister had a birthday party
for Mona, her doll. We were all invited.

When the attacks started
we didn't move.
We pretended it was چهارشنبه سوری
and the loud noises
were just fireworks.

NIGHT MIGRATIONS

Like other families
we started to leave
for the suburbs
in the evenings
and go back to our lives
in the mornings.

I didn't want to go.
If everything should be gone,
and we have to come back
to the ruins of our once house
I would rather stay and die, I announced.

If it's meant to be
we will die even in the suburbs.
This is my house
and I want to stay in my room.
And I slammed the door
the way the kids did in the movies.

There is no such a thing
as meant to be.
We choose to fight to be alive
and together as much as we can.
It was not a question.
We'll leave in an hour, my mom yelled.

POPPY PETALS

Like petals
or wildflowers in the mountain
some of our friends just left
to live in other lands
a little further
or a lot.
When my friend left one day
mom said to me
We are not rose bushes in grandma's yard
we are people
we travel
we move on
we let go
but we have memories,
stronger than roots.
We won't forget.
Keep them in your memories.
War cannot take them
away from your heart.
Can it?

RAINBOW WAR

Wind reaches out
and blows.
Somewhere nearby,
right in my city
countless leaves
orange, yellow, brown, red
purple and green
dust, pebbles,
small metal pieces
small wood chips
bird feathers
tiny human flesh pieces
flakes of skin
flying up high, dancing.
The city was bombed
a few hours ago and
it rained a few hours later,
not long . . . just for a few minutes.
It was gone before we noticed.
A long rainbow stretched
all the way across the mountains.

THE EXODUS

In the mornings
we would wait
on the corner of the sidewalk,
by Negar's apartment for all the kids to gather:
Massy, Negar, Niloufar, Leila, Suzanne, Farnaz and me

Then I would look up
to see my mom who
was always watching us through the window.
A pigeon who
lived on our balcony
between all the plants on the ledge
for years—at least that's how I remember.

Do some birds migrate because of the bombs?
I asked my mom one day.
I don't know, she replied.
I bet some of them do, I said.
They might, my mom replied.
The smart ones, I said.

THE SAME NEW DAY

War didn't stop
us from wanting a new doll.
War didn't stop
us from having birthday parties.
War didn't stop
me from wanting another baby sister or brother
(it stopped my mom from wanting another baby though).
War didn't stop
my family's passion for new plants and flowers
didn't stop my parents from
providing.

And the war didn't stop either.

We were all there
us, life, death and war
like a family
with a lot of issues.

THE GRAY

Tap-dancing
on a cracked thin glass,
some of us managed
to grow old
in a joyful fear
or perhaps in a fearful joy.
What color would my future be?
Gray
that has too much white in it?
Or maybe too much black?
I couldn't decide which was worse.

THE WAR COCOON

Like a silkworm
who has never seen
beyond the mulberry tree,
the mulberry tree
hasn't seen beyond this street.

but there comes to life
something out of a light, white
cloudy, cottony cocoon
that will fly away

with one too many silky stories
of how some made it
and some didn't.

MARCH 1988 . . . POISON GAS

b
r
e
a
t
h
l
e
s
s

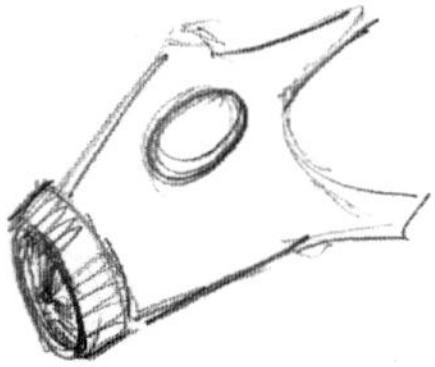

THE TURTLE AND THE MOON

Memories are wet,
gold as wheat in the field,
brown like the bag with wooden handles
and the green and red turtle that used to live on it.
The bag that secretly lived
under my bed
to comfort me through the night,
it contained water bottles, towels,
a few of my sister's and my toys,
my green metal piggy bank,
and some other useless stuff.

The tv said in an event
of chemical attack
put a wet towel on your face.

Memories are silver
cold and heavy
like a towel that has been soaked
in the lake on a cold night
with the moon dancing in the wind.

THE MISSILE

relentless,
my memories

as dandelion weeds
living in our flower bed
            that refuse to leave

the swish sound
that came with every missile
            never left either

like the bitter aftertaste
that stays long

lingering
in my mouth
in my voice
in my eyes
in my head
forever.

BIRDS LIKE BALLISTIC MISSILES

At night
we would often watch
the journey of the ballistic missiles
end over our city.
I wondered
how they travel through
stars, seas and sky
as birds do.
Only they don't have wings and shame.
Their swish sound
loud and pitchy.
Then the thunderous noise
along with the orange fire ball
in the distance
the green, blue, pink, yellow, red, gold and silver
lives that have been ruined with its arrival.
Though soon it all seemed so familiar
part of our routine
like breakfast or brushing teeth.

MANHOOD

Right after an attack

on a corner
under the Seyed Khandan bridge,
right where the taxis used to stop
there was a human piece.

burned—
a male genital organ.

It was obviously not a sign
of humankind's end

but, perhaps it was.

KARAJ, TEHRAN

The cob walls
that separated us and
the neighbor's sunflower field,
the cob wall that witnessed our fights,
friendships and imaginations,
our cries and laughters
fears and disappointments.

The short cob walls
that we used to stand by some evenings,

Army of small children.

Our parents,
sometimes a total of thirty families,
would take us all there, to Karaj,
outside of Tehran
to a friend's vacation house.
The gardens filled with fruit trees
apple, orange, plum, fig, peach, apricot, almond and walnut
and many fragile friendships.
I know one particular tree still remembers me.
(the one that uncle Bahram picked the reddest apple from,
shined it with a white cloth and gave it to me and called me
setareh, star)

We would stand there, looking up
alongside of the cob wall
entire army in a row.
The swish sound was over,
we were waiting for the missiles to land on some people's life.

Then, the entire army
would discuss the location they landed.

LEAVING

I've lived beneath my own shadow,
perhaps I still do.
Not beside it.
Not the wheat, I was the sound of the wind
in the wheat field in a hot summer.
I was the shadow of my own shadow.
Perhaps I still am.
It was no longer safe to live in our house.
It was no longer safe to live in our Tehran,
my parents decided.

THE GREEN SEDAN

We left, leaving my father behind
nothing is going to happen to him
my mother assured us.
We drove fourteen hundred kilometers.
The never-ending journey
a hole in a pocket, a bad smell stuck in nostrils.
I can still smell the inside of the car,
the cheap filthy motel, the only one available.
Not reaching wasn't hard.
what we'd left behind was beyond the imaginable.
How many families left and came back to the ruins?
How many left the ruins for the unknown?
We were the lucky ones. Perhaps we still are.
In a bright green Peykan
my sister, my mom and I,
my uncle, his in-laws and their cat
drove from north to south,
from missile rains to the turquoise of the Persian Gulf.
Supposedly more peaceful—

BITTER ME, GENEROUS PEOPLE

I was in a new school,
in a new city
under the same sky.
I went to school in a navy camp for the kids with navy parents.
The rules didn't apply in the time of war for the victims.
They accepted me, generously
I was bitter and they
were too kind to me,
it made me feel worse.
I missed my dad, who despite the stupid war
and missiles and bombs, had to work and stayed in Tehran.
I missed my friends, my home, Nader, Navid and Yeganeh,
my rest of the family.

But there we were,
a tablecloth that didn't go with the rest of the furniture.

BANDAR-ABBAS

—for Uncle Bahman

We didn't live at my uncle's house long,
each day at school though,
felt like a year.
I cried every day,
years that is!
it rained purple irises in my heart all days long.

I was now living in the city
that occupies a strategic position on the narrow *Straits of Hormoz*
like our future only narrower,
our lives on the edge

back in my uncle's house I would pretend.
After all, happiness is not an organ,
nobody is born with it
you have to earn it
like a chemistry or anthropology degree or even politics.
I would smile and play with the kids
and even watch cheesy Indian movies and laugh
from the bottom of my heart.

I would also stare at the phone
eager to hear it ring to hear my dad's voice.
I would also listen to the radio

secretly to know the areas that were hit in Tehran
nobody knew but my uncle,
he would call from work and assure me
that he spoke with my dad after every explosion.
I knew he was lying,
he knew I knew he was lying.
As if we were enjoying the lie, a joyful sin.
We were very good at pretending.

THE WAR AND THE TURQUOISE

The programs on the tv stopped

the red siren was on, along with a voice
announcing that the siren
is for the city of Bandar-Abbas
leave your houses and shelter under the palm trees the voice said.

It was dark,
the stars were shining gold and silver
like a childhood lullaby.
The sky, velvet dark blue.
We stood there under a tall palm tree
looking at each other and at the sky
and perhaps at our fate.
The air was thick and smelled humid and fearful.
My uncle didn't come home for a few days.

In the turquoise waters of the Persian Gulf
two frigates of Iran were hit,
leaving a lot of students
in my new school without fathers
only in a few hours.

Maybe it is fate.
Maybe we shouldn't have left.

They followed me:
Death, bombs, missiles, fear and the needless sense of luckiness,
lucky to be alive, lucky to have a roof,
lucky that I am not the person next to me.

We were alive.
We still are,
maybe it was fate.

FLIGHT 655—THE END

Nobody admitted the mistake.
Politicians usually don't.
That war was not a mistake.
This war isn't either!
These wars aren't
The ones that haven't happened yet,
won't be mistakes either.

War is a necessity
to sell guns.
They are calculated, measured
precisely like beehives
They won't stop, they come back
like weeds in our grass.
Bombs will continue
like rose petals in full bloom
that drop with a summer breeze.

As an adult,
I refuse to accept it!

But life goes on.
Birds fly high,
seeds become orange,
and yellow, red and green tomatoes turn.

I remember crisp, skinny Persian cucumbers,
Tabriz salty cheese,
cilantro and scallions, limes and olives,
and the smell of saffron rice from my mom's kitchen.

ABOUT THE AUTHOR

Pantea Amin Tofangchi is an Iranian-American poet, writer, and graphic designer. She writes poems (in English), essays, stories and plays (mostly in Persian.) Her work has been published in Ploughshares, Little Patuxent Review, Welter Atlanta Review—in which she won the International Merit Award—and other journals. She was selected as a finalist for The National Poetry Series' 2016 and Georgia Poetry Prize 2018.

ACKNOWLEDGMENTS

I am indebted to many people for their advice, support and encouragement. This book has lived inside me and will live forever like a deep scar one carries to the end of life. My dear friends and family, you have helped me give this true story a new form that can live far beyond me. A form that can be read, shared, held, written on, carried, slept with, folded, bent, or even recycled, not just by me but by millions like me who believe that war doesn't bring peace and is never the answer.

I want to thank my family: my father for always encouraging me to write more and to dig deeper, my mom who teaches me patience and love every single day, and my amazing sister who is the true meaning of *pure*.

Bahareh Negahban, Laura Shovan and Judith Krummeck, I am forever grateful for your unwavering support and wisdom. Ebrahim Afshar, if you only knew how much I appreciate everything you taught me. Special thanks to my University of Baltimore friends, mentors and teachers. You saw this book before I started writing it. I cannot thank you enough. Amoo Ali and Khaleh Soody, now I know why you left, so that years later I can come to you, and thousands of miles and oceans away from home still smell home. Thank you for all your love and support. You are *satri barjeste az zendegie man*.

I am genuinely grateful to Mason Jar, working with you was an incredible journey. Celeste, thank you for all your brilliant editing. Ian, I am so glad my book was in your capable hands. Michael, you are a true bro. Thank you Ashley and Heather, all I can say is: *It marked the edge of one of many circles.*

And last, how can I ever thank my best friend and my husband Shahriar, without whom many things would have been impossible, including this book. Thank you for your thoughtfulness and patience. Thank you for reading all the too many drafts, you even drew them.

I thank you all deeply: for all that is noble in *ba hameye vojood*.

NOTES:

Khorramshahr

A port and city in southwestern Iran on the west bank of the Kārūn River where it meets the Arvand Rud (Shatt al-Arab). The city has been in existence since the time of Alexander the Great. Khorramshahr was a prosperous trading center during the Seleucid period and through the Sāsānian and Islamic periods. During World War II, it was connected with the Trans-Iranian Railway which brought many improvements, and, by the 1960s, had become an important commercial port. However, the port sustained great loses during Iran-Iraq War—first when it captured by Iraq in 1980 and subsequently when it was recaptured by Iran in 1982. By 1986 the recorded population of Khorramshahr was zero. Following the end of the Iran-Iraq War, the city was rebuilt and the population returned close to pre-war levels. The port was partly rebuilt and ship traffic returned in the 1990s.

The title مرگ قناری در قفس (the death of canary in cage) is from the poem "A Teardrop for the Passage of History" by Fereydoon Moshiri, one of the prominent contemporary Persian poets who wrote poems in both modern and classic styles. A stanza of that poem is written as an inline dedication in Persian at the beginning of the poem. Here is a rough translation of that excerpt:

...Suppose the death of canary in cage is not even a death

Suppose not even one stem of flower has ever bloomed in the world,
suppose the forests were desert from day one,
in the silent desert,
within people so patient with all the sufferings,
kindness is dying, love is dying
humanity is dying...

Sound barrier

When jet pilots fly faster than sound travels, it creates a sonic boom that is as loud as a bomb explosion. We were so used to both that I could tell them apart as a kid.

چهارشنبه سوری in the poem "The Emerald Night" is an Iranian festival of the fire dance celebrated on the eve of the last Wednesday of the year, of ancient Zoroastrian origin. It is the first festivity of Nowruz, the Iranian New Year.

About the last poem

Iran Air Flight 655 was a civilian jet airliner shot down by US missiles on July 3, 1988 as it flew over the Strait of Hormuz at the end of the Iran–Iraq War. The aircraft was an Airbus operated by Iran Air. It was flying from Bandar Abbas, Iran to Dubai, United Arab Emirates. While flying in Iranian airspace over Iran's territorial waters in the Persian Gulf on its usual flight path, it was destroyed by a United States Navy guided missile cruiser. All 290 on-board, including 66 children and 16 crew, perished.

The incident is ranked ninth among the deadliest disasters in aviation history.

According to the United States Government, the crew identified the Iranian Airbus A300 as an attacking F-14. The US supported Iraq during the Iran-Iraq war. The support included several billion dollars' worth of economic aid, the sale of dual-use technology, military intelligence, and special operations training.

In 1996, the United States and Iran reached "an agreement in full and final settlement of all disputes, differences, claims, counterclaims" relating to the incident at the International Court of Justice. As part of the settlement, the United States agreed to pay $61.8 million, an average of about $213.000 per passenger, in compensation to the families of the Iranian victims. However, the United States has never admitted responsibility, nor apologized to Iran. As a matter of fact, based on the documentary by National Geographic, the crew was greeted and welcomed by balloons and flowers and they were treated like heroes when they reached the San Diego harbor. Shortly after, the Iran-Iraq war was ended.

OTHER TITLES FROM MASON JAR PRESS

After the Rapture
novella by Nancy Stohlman

lesser american boys
short stories by Zach VandeZande

JERKS
short stories by Sara Lippmann

The Monotonous Chaos of Existence
short stories by Hisham Bustani

Peculiar Heritage
poetry DeMisty D. Bellinger

Call a Body Home
short stories chapbook by Michael Alessi

The Horror is Us
an anthology of horror fiction edited by Justin Sanders

Suppose Muscle Suppose Night Suppose This in August
memoir by Danielle Zaccagnino

Learn more at masonjarpress.com